SMART ABOUT
Art

PABLO PICASSO
BREAKING ALL THE RULES

by
Simon Packard

written + illustrated by TRUE KELLEY

Grosset & Dunlap • New York

For Jamaica and Jessamine Kelley—T.K.

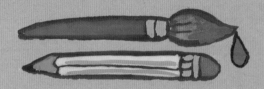

Library of Congress Cataloging-in-Publication Data

Kelley, True.
    Pablo Picasso : breaking all the rules / written and illustrated by True Kelley.
        p. cm.
    Summary: Examines the life and work of Picasso, discussing the different styles in which he worked.
        1. Picasso, Pablo, 1881–1973—Juvenile literature. 2. Artists—France—Biography—Juvenile literature. [1. Picasso, Pablo, 1881–1973. 2. Artists. 3. Painting, French. 4. Painting, Modern—20th century. 5. Art appreciation.] I. Title.
    N6853.P5 K45 2002
    709'.2—dc21

                                                            2002004665

ISBN 978-0-448-42862-8 (pbk)   K L M N O P Q R S T

From the desk of
Ms. Brandt

Dear Class,

Our unit on famous artists is almost over. I hope that you enjoyed it as much as I did.

I am excited to read your reports. Here are some questions that you may want to think about:

🎨 Why did you pick your artist?

🎨 If you could ask your artist 3 questions, what would they be?

🎨 Did you learn anything that really surprised you?

Good luck and have fun!

Ms. Brandt

THE TRUTH ABOUT THIS REPORT!

To tell the truth, I wasn't crazy about the idea of doing Picasso for my report. My favorite painter is Monet, but my twin brother, Steven, already took him. My parents have Picasso posters and prints and books all over our house so he was the easiest artist for me to write about. (Sorry, Ms. Brandt! But when I started this report, I didn't like his art that much. But now I do.)

My dad with one of our Posters by you-know-who.

Pablo Picasso was born in southern Spain on October 25, 1881. He could draw before he could talk. His first words were *"Piz! Piz!"* which means "Pencil! Pencil!" in Spanish. His full name was Pablo Diego José Francisco de Paula Juan Nepomuceno María de los Remedios Cipriano de la Santísima Trinidad Ruiz Picasso.

I'm glad he shortened his name to Pablo Picasso or signing a painting would have been a major problem.

The Boy Genius

Pablo's father was a painter and art teacher. He wanted Pablo to be an artist. By the time Pablo was 14, everybody already thought he was an artistic genius.

When his dad saw how well Pablo could paint, he gave him all his own paints and brushes and never painted again.

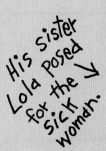

His sister Lola posed for the sick woman. →

The doctor → *is his dad.*

Sketch for *Science and Charity* by Pablo Picasso. 1897. Museo Picasso, Barcelona, Spain/Index/Bridgeman Art Library.

Here's Pablo's sketch for a painting he did when he was only 16. The painting won a prize. Pablo beat some of the best artists in Spain.

Picasso left home to go to art school in Madrid. But he skipped class a lot. He was getting tired of being told how to paint. He just wanted to do it his own way.

When he was just starting out Pablo roomed with his friend Carles Casagemas. They were so poor that Picasso painted furniture and bookcases on the walls so their apartment didn't look so bare!

The BLUE PERIOD

Paris, France, was the cool place to be for artists, so Pablo and Carles Casagemas soon moved there. Picasso liked Paris. But his friend Carles was very unhappy. He had girl trouble, and in 1901 he killed himself. Picasso was very sad, and it showed in his paintings.

I think Picasso felt really sorry for this old guy.

The clothes are so ragged.

Is the guitar player crying?

> It was thinking of Casagemas that made me start painting in blue.

Picasso painted beggars and prisoners and tramps and drunks. The blue paint he used made the paintings even sadder.

Pablo's "blue" paintings didn't sell very well. Who would want such depressing pictures on their walls? Even Pablo's dad thought he was wasting his talent.

Here's my own sad painting in blue. It's about when our cat died.

TIMES ARE FINE

Pablo fell in love in 1904. Pablo and his girlfriend were happy even though they were poor. Picasso started using new colors and his paintings looked happier. Some people call this Picasso's Rose Period, but I don't know why. Most of the paintings weren't just pink.

Pablo's apartment was a big mess. (Sort of like my room, I guess.) Picasso often worked all night by oil lamp. In winter it got so cold that by morning cups of leftover tea had frozen.

Pablo's pet white mouse lived in a drawer, safe from cats.

Pablo's big dog, Frika

An American woman named Gertrude Stein was living in Paris with her brother Leo. Gertrude was a poet and was one of the first people who liked Pablo's paintings.

Lots of artists and poets were always hanging out at Gertrude Stein's house. Picasso also met the painter Henri Matisse there. Picasso thought Matisse was the greatest painter around. They became friends for life.

Self-portrait by Pablo Picasso. 1907. Nimatallah / Art Resource, NY.

Here's what Picasso looked like in those days. Gertrude's brother Leo joked that he wouldn't lend Picasso a book because he might burn holes in it with his staring eyes.

In 1906 Picasso did a portrait of Gertrude Stein, but he just couldn't get the face right. She sat for him 80 times! Picasso gave up for the summer, but when he began again he did her face from memory. People said it didn't look like her. Gertrude loved it.

I think Gertrude looks like a mountain. Picasso made her look very solid and strong.

Painted in 1906

And Now For Something COMPLETELY DIFFERENT...

Les Demoiselles d'Avignon by Pablo Picasso. 1907. Museum of Modern Art, New York, USA/Lauros-Giraudon-Bridgeman Art Library.

painted in 1907

Picasso saw some African art like this mask in a museum. Look! It shows up in this painting!

← Her head is on backwards!

I **don't** like this !!!

It doesn't look finished! The women are sharp and weird looking!

Picasso took months to paint this picture after many, many sketches (809!). He did it only a year after he painted Gertrude. I can't believe the same person did both. But Pablo was always trying out new ways of painting. He didn't mind breaking the rules. Most people thought paintings should look real. They were shocked by this picture of five women. I can see why. The women seem to be breaking up in pieces...but wait until you see what comes next!

CUBISM-

The painter Georges Braque was also breaking all the rules of art. He and Picasso both started painting with only a few colors and breaking up the pictures into cubes or geometric shapes. They were trying to paint things from all angles at once: from the front; from the sides.

This is a portrait of a man who owned an art gallery. He was one of the only people who liked this style which is called Cubism.

Can you see his face? Hands? Clothes? Bottle? Glass? It's like a puzzle!

I paint objects as I think them, not as I see them.

PICASSO'S PAINTING

DARE TO BE SQUARE

Braque and Picasso worked together for five years. They saw each other every day. They went on vacations together. Braque said he and Picasso were like roped-together mountaineers. They were sort of like my twin brother and me—they thought alike. They invented Cubism. Steven and I haven't invented much yet.

Man with a Guitar by Georges Braque. 1914. Musée National d'Art Moderne, Paris, France/Lauros-Giraudon-Bridgeman Art Library.

BRAQUE'S PAINTING

CUBISM!

Braque

Picasso

Me

I'm hungry!

Steven

There's supposed to be a man and a guitar there somewhere.

COLLAGE

Here's my own collage. →

Picasso and Braque began sticking things like cloth or pieces of paper or even trash on their paintings. They also used stencils and lettering. This new kind of art was called "collage", which comes from a French word meaning "to stick."

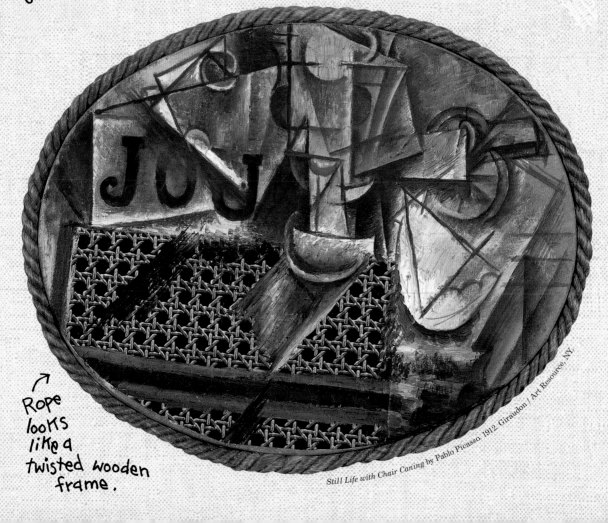

↗ Rope looks like a twisted wooden frame.

Still Life with Chair Caning by Pablo Picasso. 1912. Giraudon / Art Resource, NY.

Picasso went to Rome to design some sets and costumes for a ballet. He had never even seen a ballet before! He fell in love with one of the ballerinas, Olga. He married her a year later. When Picasso painted this portrait of Olga most Cubists thought he was a sellout, because he was painting in an old-fashioned way. But he was just doing his own thing again. He wanted to paint Olga this way—so he did!

Portrait of Olga on an Armchair by Pablo Picasso. 1917. Giraudon / Art Resource, NY.

He used a photo to paint her. I bet she didn't want to sit for him long.

← Look! It's not finished.

Picasso was quite a ladies' man. Turn the page and see!

PABLO'S LOVE LIFE

In his long life, Picasso had lots of girlfriends and wives and four children. In each picture I put the year they met.

Fernande

1905

Marie-Thérèse

Maya

1935

1927

Dora

1936

I was pretty surprised to find out that Picasso was short — only 5'3".

Eva

1911

Olga

Paulo

1921

1917

Françoise

Claude Paloma

1944   1947   1949

Jacqueline

1953

But art was always Pablo's first love.

PICASSO PAINTS

> Painting is stronger than I am; it makes me do what it wants.

Pablo painted both the painting on this page and the one on the next page in 1921. Look how different they are! This one below is crazy looking, like a puzzle with pieces in the wrong places. Can you tell what it is? The answer is at the bottom of the page!

Les Trois Musiciens by Pablo Picasso. 1921. Museum of Modern Art, New York, USA/Bridgeman Art Library.

There are three musicians. Two of them are clowns and one is a monk. There's a dog, too.

Gertrude? →

The thick legs of the women → reminded Picasso of happy days as a child. He'd crawl under the dinner table and look at everybody's ankles!

Three Women at the Fountain by Pablo Picasso. 1921. Museum of Modern Art, New York, USA/Bridgeman Art Library.

This painting looks like some of the statues Picasso saw when he was in Rome. By 1921 Picasso was the top artist of the day. The Man! Even though he was rich and famous, he never stopped making all kinds of art. He was always ready to try something new.

WAR

In 1937 Picasso painted his angriest painting ever. It is a picture of a town in Spain called Guernica. It was bombed during the Spanish Civil War. It is scary if you look at it very long. Innocent people are dying. It could be about any war.

A screaming mother ↓ holds her dead baby.

The dying horse's tongue looks like a knife. ↓

why is there a lightbulb? ↙

In June of 1940, during World War II, the German Nazis took over Paris. Picasso wouldn't leave, even though he could have. The French people were very proud of that. I think he was quite brave. Food was scarce. When he was hungry, he painted sausages and leeks. It was hard to get art supplies. Picasso somehow kept working.

There's a cut-off arm holding a sword. And a cut-off head! It's HORRIBLE!

Guernica by Pablo Picasso. 1937. Giraudon / Art Resource, NY.

It's 12 feet high and 25 feet long!

PEACE

In 1944 the Nazis were run out of Paris. It was a free city again. American soldiers there said that Picasso and the Eiffel Tower were the sights they most wanted to see. So Picasso gave tours of his studio.

When Picasso's daughter was born in 1949, he named her Paloma, which means "dove" in Spanish.

My brother says my dove↑ looks like a pigeon!

After living through so many wars, Picasso wanted to work for peace. In 1949 Picasso made a poster of a dove for the Peace Congress. Today the dove is a symbol for peace all over the world.

After the war Picasso moved to southern France with his new girlfriend. They bought an old perfume factory to use as a sculpture studio. They had a son, Claude, in 1947 and a daughter, Paloma, in 1949. Picasso was a happy family man. He played with his kids and painted pictures of them, too. There was a pottery factory in the town where they lived, and Picasso began making and decorating plates, vases and pots. He made 2,000 pieces in one year! Go Picasso!

SCULPTURE

Picasso was not just a painter and a potter. He made sculptures in bronze. He liked to make them out of things he found around the place.

I think Picasso loved junk!

You should be able to take a piece of wood and find it's a bird.

BAAH!

Can you see the two old milk pitchers?

The stomach is a basket.

The Goat by Pablo Picasso. 1950. Giraudon / Art Resource, NY.

More and more Picasso made surprising and funny art! I really like these collage-sculptures. He was much more playful than most great artists. I think Picasso had a good sense of humor. I bet his kids liked these sculptures of a little girl jumping rope and a mother pushing a baby carriage.

Girl Skipping by Pablo Picasso. 1950. CNAC/MNAM/Dist. Réunion des Musées Nationaux / Art Resource, NY.

Woman with Baby Carriage by Pablo Picasso. 1950. Hirshhorn Museum and Sculpture Garden, Smithsonian Institution, Gift of Joseph. H. Hirshhorn, 1972. Photograph by Lee Stalsworth.

THE YOUNG OLD MAN

I have less and less time and yet, I have more and more to say.

In 1954 Henri Matisse died. Picasso was 73 and was afraid he was running out of time, too. His wife and children had left him. So what did he do?

⟶ This is his studio.

Picasso's studio (circa 1955). Hulton Archive / Getty Images.

Picasso worked even harder. He found a new girlfriend. Picasso got married again! He was 80.

me, swimming (with Picasso!)

Picasso swimming. Hulton Archive / Getty Images.

Look at this guy! He's still swimming and having fun! By now Picasso was a living legend.

On his 85th birthday museums in Paris had shows of Picasso's work. There were 1,000 pieces of art. It was hard to believe one person could have done it all!

And there's more!

MY FAVORITE PICASSO

Man With a Straw Hat and an Ice Cream Cone by Pablo Picasso. 1938.
Réunion des Musées Nationaux / Art Resource, NY.

← Nice hat, but the guy needs a shave!

← Vanilla ice cream?

Maybe he's blue because he's cold from eating the ice cream.

I have this poster in my room, so now there isn't a single room in our house without a Picasso in it! Not even our bathroom!

This is a Picasso painting with lots of blue in it, but it doesn't look sad at all. It's my favorite. I think Picasso liked ice cream as much as I do. (He painted it in some of his other pictures, too.) When I look at Picasso's work, I feel like I want to paint or make stuff myself.